Swimming with Dolphins

Swimming with Dolphins

Adrian Oktenberg

Lewisburg
Bucknell University Press
London: Associated University Presses

Associated University Presses
440 Forsgate Drive
Cranbury, NJ 08512

Associated University Presses
16 Barter Street
London WC1A 2AH, England

Associated University Presses
P.O. Box 338, Port Credit
Mississauga, Ontario
Canada L5G 4L8

Library of Congress Cataloging-in-Publication Data

Oktenberg, Adrian, 1947–
    Swimming with dolphins / Adrian Oktenberg.
        p.   cm. — (Bucknell series in contemporary poetry)
    ISBN 0-8387-5516-X (alk. paper)
    I. Title.   II. Series.

PS3565.K75.S95   2002
811′.54—dc21   2001043191

For my Friends

Jan Freeman
Ruth Gundle
Aleta Mason
Ellen Yaroshefsky

*Stand face to face with me
as a friend would*
                    —Sappho

Contents

IV. Green Sun

V. Catastrophe Theory

VI. *Hyakutake*

Acknowledgments

Thanks to the editors of the publications in which the following poems first appeared, often in somewhat different form:

Americas Review: "Argentine Memory"
Bay Windows: "Sunday Morning"
Blueline: "Gravity"
Luna: "The Creation" and "To Amelia, from Dob"
Nimrod: "Seed," "Rock," "Stream," "Cloud," and "Beach," from *North*
Prairie Schooner: "Days of 1992" and "Lament, After Liu Yung"
Primavera: "The House"
Quarterly West: "Asters, September"
The American Voice: "Eating Truffles with Colette" and "Woman Embrac-
    ing Tree"
The Devil's Millhopper: "Whose crystalline single words," "Aurora . . .
    chorus," "Cleis! Daughter!", "Sun setting behind translucent blades,"
    "Aphrodite . . . rich-worked throne," "The moon has set, and the Plei-
    ades," "My darling Atthis," "Soft . . . Eros," "Women working," "Light
    fades from sea crest," "To me . . . a god," "Girl rising from surf"

"Night Pee" appeared in Gerry Gomez Pearlberg, ed., *Queer Dog: Homo/
Pup/Poems* (San Francisco: Cleis Press, 1997). "Woman Embracing Tree,"
"Night Pee," and "The Garden" appeared in a chapbook, *Drawing in the
Dirt* (Brockport, NY: Malachite & Agate, 1997). "Woman Embracing Tree"
also appeared in Frederick Smock, ed., *The American Voice Anthology of
Poetry* (Louisville: University Press of Kentucky, 1998). "Hyakutake" ap-
peared in Robert McGovern and Stephen Haven, ed., *And What Rough
Beast: Poems at the End of the Century* (Ashland, OH: The Ashland Poetry
Press, 1999).

Thanks to the editors of *Americas Review* for awarding that journal's poetry
prize for "Argentine Memory." Thanks also to Centrum, the Massachusetts
Cultural Council, the Montana Artist's Refuge, the Helene Wurlitzer
Foundation of New Mexico, and the Stadler Center for Poetry at Bucknell
University for generous assistance. Thanks to Ann R. Stokes for hospitality

at Welcome Hill, and to Nick and Elspeth Macdonald for the extraordinary gift of Slough Pond. Special thanks to Frederick Smock, formerly of *The American Voice*, and Marianne Milton, formerly of *Malachite & Agate*, for their support of my work. I am immensely grateful to Nicole Cooley, Jan Freeman, Tsipi Keller, Henry Lyman, Karl Patten, Carol Potter, Peggy Shumaker, Pamela Stewart, and Ruth Stone, each of whom has given attention, assistance, kindness, and understanding.

Swimming with Dolphins

Aphrodite of the sparkling eye
rose from the sea
extended her arm   slender as a dolphin's arc
from shoulder to wrist and open hand
touched her fingertip   to Sappho's finger
        quickened her
to desire and sing of desire
to bear her leather phallus
        at the pit and summit of joy

There and then   the world began

I.
Touch

First, the bank account must allow.
Truffles must be "eaten like potatoes,"
in quantities one delights in, or not at all.
Then, one must wait, until after the coming
of the frost, when Périgord delivers
its finest. Colette alone can clean them,
for cleaning, she insists, is itself an art.
She browns shards of bacon
in a heavy pan, adds pepper, salt,
and half a bottle of dry white wine.
When at last it bubbles fully, she throws
in the truffles, all at once with a flourish,
raising an arm in salute like a trapézière.
Immediately there rises and spreads through the house
that divine and sexual odor.
The scented sauce is served separately,
hot in port glasses. There was also a time,
just one night of perfection at the Marquise's.
We hid truffles under the ashes.
It was a simple midnight supper, quite
like a family, but with something singular
about the atmosphere, the repartée, the eyes.

She came daily, bringing corn,
and hardly spoke, but held you
at a distance, not knowing your loneliness
craved connection. So you walked
into the desert with your dog
and spoke to the dog and the stars.
You knew your increasing sorrow
would never find an answer there, or clasp of compassion,
nothing but your own voice
echoing off mountain walls, the ceilings of stars.
Returning, it thinned to less than a whisper.
In despair you fell on your knees and hugged your dog,
her eyes on you, the smell of her skin
warm as longed-for touch, sun on desert floor.

I lie under the length, the light weight of her body
and her breasts fall into my hands. I warm them, I stroke,
I give them the full extent of my lips, my mouth opens in surprise,
my tongue is shy at first but then sees no need for foolishness, begins
to make them familiar, to map them slowly, slower still
to explore the ways of their swelling, their curves and shadowy passages,
their volcanic cones, the mysterious cleft between.
I press my face between her breasts, inhale and cup them
in my hands and bring them close, hear the pulse,
the roar of ocean in the shells of my ears.
Willingly I become blind, touch is my finest medium
and I also smell, as in a forest one smells the odor of roots, at her
    breastbone,
and the idea of moss, the dark and moist sublime, comes to me.
I hear our noises, some tart, some sweet, as we move together
and the small noises of night, house-noises, tree-noises,
animal-noises. Outside, the moon: I feel it poring gravely over us.
And I bend. In my mind I am kneeling. My lips, shaped in awe,
hands cupped, palms shining.

WOMAN EMBRACING TREE

You go out quietly, and I know where
you are going. I followed you once.
To the woods, to find the white birch

split five ways at the ground, the tree
you think is a secret, that holds your secrets,
like Shiva, in its numerous arms.

I saw you stand,
face to face as a friend would,
but at a slight distance, with respect.

Then you stepped forward
in a measured way, as if
at a ceremony,

embraced the white birch,
cheek on bark, coolly resting.
Birch bent to you, listening.

You said a few words, held
the tree in your arms for a moment,
stepped back shyly.

I know, you don't have to tell me.
I myself once had a high pasture,
and then a river, many years ago.

Night Pee

Your house seems so empty without you,
but when I find the key and enter
the rooms are warm, as if they have retained
your body and the breath of animals moving
through them. The dogs greet me with hallelujahs
of barking and dog-brouhaha, approaching
and backing off and coming, each pressing
her polar bear head against my thigh.

I have come to walk them—delayed in town,
you called to sweetly ask this favor.
I don't mind when you ask like that.
Two feet of snow on the ground,
no traffic on the road, and branches creak above us.
Otherwise the night is silent, and stars shimmer
satellite greetings in faint colors.
I stand in misery, hating this cold, curse
my forgotten gloves, but the dogs don't mind.
They wear their heavy coats and no boots, and they ignore m
busy tracing out whatever's so interesting
under the snow.

Dot stops, sniffs, digs fast with her paw,
but I'll never know what she finds there. When
at last Emma pauses and casually drops her hips
to pee, meanwhile looking around
in case any morsel like chipmunk should appear,
I feel grateful. She turns and runs the long
plowed driveway with such exuberance and speed
it forces me to murmur salute. I feel my face crack
when I move my mouth to speak. My voice
sounds loud against the branches of stars and trees.
Sure enough, in a minute, Dot pees too,
and together they crowd against the door
like riders rushing to board. Each takes up
a station on a different rug as I walk around
the rooms, turning on lights for you,

25

tuning the radio to jazz for them.
I tell them you'll be back quite soon, all's well.
Tomorrow is New Year's Eve,
summer and all its smells will be upon us soon.

II.
Stellar Aqua

She too lay in the dune,
her face, like mine, half hidden,
resting on brown arms.
Our bodies absorbed the heat. We breathed in
     unison.
Waves broke in unison. Neither of us spoke.

To you who know the sea only from shore,
who gaze as if waves were wind-blown stands of grass,
whose feet grow more and more embedded, immobile in the sucking sand
at surf-edge, I say *immerse.*

The fused seam where water meets sky
and color dissolves into light
and all is distance, brilliance, longing
for that horizon, an ache.
Aren't you rooted in soil? Ruled by desire?
Light-years are a measure of distance, not time.

Ocean more ancient than an Aztec mask,
a human skull inlaid with turquoise and jet,
recalls the lust of death.
The sea loves to kill: more, adores it,
violence cores it.
Death by drowning lacks peace.
At these depths bleached faces greet you—
Shelley, Virginia, Hart—
features smooth as driftwood.
The sea-roar calls, subsumes all will,
master glitterer, urger, drug.
Resolute, knowing the worst, you may still
     succumb.

Restless ranges of silver, salt, and sky
perform a constant tumult in the eye.
Gaze until the eye goes dim, cloudy
among such brightness. Unfamiliar perspectives
jar the old arrangements, knowledge unravels,

the surfline that advanced with menace
now casts a lifeline to draw you in.
The coast falls away behind you, less
and less essential, already dead,
while the sea is alive, coming closer, closer in.
Not fear of risk but dilution claims you,
the enticing promise of fluidity,
the alchemist body transmuted, trembling
and tumbling with the universe, one.

You have waited for this chance.

I am the surf
curling around your knees, I am your sea-horse lover,
acolyte, I kiss your feet.

I crawl into bed beside you
and you turn to me in sleep, wrapping your leg
around my waist, letting your arm fall
across my back. I slip my thigh
between yours, put my arms around you,
one stretched out under your neck, the other
along the back of your hip. Your buttocks curve
under my hand. You murmur something
I can't quite hear. I sigh and groan a little.
We sleep.

Come, let it come, slip into water without a splash,
live no longer a vertical but a horizontal life,
immerse in the present, fuse with neither past nor future,
refocus desire, memory, thought, be confused and confounded.
Down far and farther, plunge where color dissolves into ink, find the
    space
long before mountains emerged from the sea.
There was water
before you were a body, a streak.

Drop like water into water,
let your body go unarmored, lose its weight,
be astonished, be humble,
you are human, surprise becomes you.

Terra firma, gone, speech, gone,
replaced by wordless touch, movement, otherworldly light,
the curly kale-leaf edge of the old world
fallen off, the new one green and blue and as riveted with light
as everything we knew but now find changed.

We sink like tons, shocked, frozen, panicked,
thrown with the surf, jettisoned, choked, glazed with fear,
until we fall unhooked unanchored,
let the body go.

> The sense of the earth falls away, gravity
> now feels arbitrary.
> Awkward and temporal,
> we assume amorphous shapes,
> charge the depths, down,
> down, down into the shock of noon,
> inhale deeply, plunge without anchor, beyond any
>   chains,
> green, iridescent water . . . .

Anemones extend their arms, reveal coral fans
swaying in silence, labia part
rapt to sensation, eyes wide, unblinking
in absorption, now we can hear the brain coral think.
Ruminations of fish, their flashes, talented schools,
susurrations of seaweeds and sponges, cries and songs of seals,
whales, manatees, dolphins, make perfect sense.
We know and feel everything:
language softly and brilliantly colored,
ciphered speech comes in the whorls of our ear,
we're untroubled, at ease.

Arrived unseen
the dolphins surround us,
and when the rhythm of our mutual pleasure
sounds in their ears, they slip by
and under and through our bodies, blue bodies tumbling in blue light
twined in double and triple chains that open and come apart,
suddenly single, becoming individual, suddenly, *that smile*,
and rising toward the surface they break for the sun
or the moon, with shimmering spans, mists, sprays,

water falling into water, bodies leaping and diving,
stellar aqua plumbed.
We swim, bodies twinned, and breathe together
with the ease of those born to it, for this
we have risked. We have chosen it.
You enter and leave me repeatedly and I writhe
one hand above my head, one scoring your back.
I suck your nipple, it buds in my mouth,
my tongue implores, your fingers grow sweet,
skins slippery, lips part,
opened, the living coral fan unfolds.

Whose mouth in whose whole, mouth, palm, part,
exploding every part of the surface, skin, orifice,
breaking through for the deep, stunning
the sonar interior skin, illuminating the cave, the core,
ultramarine breasts heavy and light, each one
cupped in each hand, whisper
every sound and particle of the pleasurable,
seek the translucent water, brighter light,
and the shimmer and reach of the whole surface
spreads lights across the colors of the palpable,
ebony, shell-pink, blue-tinged, gleaming,
plural the shirred cries crying,
multiples purifying.

Nosed between the startling globes
of buttocks, bottlenose dolphin, green,
spotted dolphin, silver white and gray,
social, protective, funny, smart,
not solemn, but comic, intuitive, innocent.

One the keeper, one the guide,
one that has been purified,
one that serves as pivotal pole
around which others twirl and whorl,
one teaches, one plays,
one—the smallest—newly born to praise,
one searches, depth astronomer,
one the expert fathomer,
one rises, another sinks,

a gymnast executes a somersault, almost winks,
a bold one's velvet nose implores my thigh,
moves higher—noses, smiles, multiply,
all wheel, all spoke . . .

In this exuberant language I badinage,
let myself play into it, animate, you breathe in your dream,
exhale a more fluent speech, language created of difference,
language of those who have no shame, no law of the forbidden, no code
    of silence,
language that speaks openly of desire, hunger, need, protection, comfort,
language clean as dune, as grains of sand washed with pure water,
clear as an azure egg of sky with water running fast beneath it,
in which all that is seen and spoken is freely seen and spoken.
A life taken whole, lived in the open, subject only
to this geography, water, water, land, sky,
life fully seen and recognized, spoken, freely reported, understood.

I am tumbling in silent laughter,
the dark comes from the distance
and touches a sliver, the merest coin-edge, of light,
something lighter touches my skin, just touches, the lightest touch,
airy, faint, barely there, a nose, a nostril, a rose's aroma
swimming there, parts, centers, spurs open
anemone, unfolds wind-flower.

I am a spiral falling, letting go, pressure increases, presses
into the hollows, the shallows, locates the cave the secret the hidden the
    core
the great Egyptian eye of desire, explores, examines, circles, slows,
holds, and serenely and with dignity and gravity, knows.

And if we lie, humbled in each other's arms,
I'll swear by my goddess Aphrodite,
by all that is sacred to me I'll swear,
I've touched and been marked by grace:
the goddesses having granted me this.

We are pulled toward sky, cirrus and cerulean,
sun cradled in horizon, where the sea resumes its great silence.

Stars are strung above the harbor
where boats with furled sails come to mooring,
    gunnels shining.
The vin gai and triste of summer music
swirls again. Gravely, as after a long time together,
I take you in my arms and we dance.

III.
Naked Women Swimming in Coves

Here you will find no mention of Priam

                                    earlier poets have left accounts

the pit
the heart
the peach

                                        whose crystalline single words
                                    translucent   drops of water

Nectar poured into golden

                        enticement with her hands

Aurora   chorus
Eos   dawn.

                    earlier, golden and azure

                                        hair

Cleis! Daughter! Do not fold your arms across your breasts

    your foremost secret

                                   swift sandals
                                      on rocks.

sun setting behind translucent blades

                                              pines

                                          paler than grass

                                      charcoal and red chalk
What woven pattern might my love want   for her floor?

The fingertips that brush my wrist

                    42

                              who could stop my breath

                         as if I were a girl!

Like the foolish bird that bathes in sand

My hands   slip down

                                        I can't help myself

Aphrodite

                        figures on a red ground

She has no art to deny

           and I

             strict

           in the pursuit of love

"Give her a song that seduces,"

Aphrodite   rich-worked throne

make little flames and launch them on the sea

in the month of Geraistos

My darling Atthis

to look at her in lamplight
her gown loosed from about her shoulders

                              open
                              the fig

flashing in the curl of the wave

A bridle of sweet-smelling leather

silver

leather phallus

women working
half water, half whirlwind

                                                  looping purple ribbons

          the aroma of pine nuts roasting   chilled wine,

                                                       when she arrives.

To me   a god who sits
at your side and hears you speak

my heart has ceased
blood pounds in my ears

                                   grass,

but for your sake I

                Aphrodite   of the plunging horses

Be gracious   50

            on one who falls nightly in and out of love

Tired of life, and not yet twenty-two!

         and when she has done for you

What then?

Light fades from sea crest

who sleeps   shells,
who sleeps   nets,
                              darling Atthis,
                          at distant Sardis
                          Cypriot copper,

                                                        coast.

Among Lydian women

        did you offer your thighs?

The moon   shows only her slender waist

The most devoted
        from Miletus
        from Phocaea
        from Colophon

So I am your "darling girl"!

your kisses suggest one

                               "who knows what she wants."

But when I whisper, "

                            you clear your throat and cough

Swallows, still your talk!
Let me sleep

                    that a dream may lock me in her arms.

Sun   softness,

sun and the beaten hardness
Sun   song.

It's no use
I can't finish my weaving

Blame Aphrodite

beautiful, it blew all around her

and over her shoulders

Gongyla, I ask you to wear
a sheaf of lilies   cloud

                    and I am glad, though we quarreled

In the month when the Pleiades has set

                                                    when she is roundest

and lights the earth with her silver

yet it is only sleep

          that falls on her mouth   her breast,

On soft mats   lamps

        girls with all they most wished for
lying beside them

                                                    dawn

                                                  grain.

Certainly we kissed

     in the shadows of dunes
     the thresholds of houses

Entangled

               in cypress-shadow

                   under the wide cloak

                       by stars

                   tossing pine torches

from the headland into the sea

I'll bring white violets   narcissus,

roses

     roses, and these I'll twine

I swear by Timo's curls
             for   Heliodora   by Antocleia's smile,

                                        64

                                                            I swear it.

Come quickly, Atthis!

                              your pitcher with the lovely mouth

More beautiful than a fleet of warships blackening the sea

66

More beautiful than a fleet of warships blackening the sea

Musa the dark-eyed, the singing

                        her thigh on mine

Musa who was so much loved

Because we knew the pillows would say, "I know," we slept without them

    our names were linked in unlikely rooms

Let them say

                                nevertheless,

girl rising from surf

"Go," you said, "Do not be unhappy

                              lovers

                    never

          I shall come."

IV.
Green Sun

Seed

I can't look at all at these green hills
without thinking of him, waiting
in stillness for the scrawny winter dawn,
or look at the colors, gorgeous and decayed,
of leaves heaped upon each other,
or catch the flash of red-winged blackbirds
scudding in weeds, or feel the presence
of a stand of birches in snow at twilight,
or watch the slow danse macabre of the seasons,
its turning, returning, rebirth,
without thinking of one
who went to fetch water for tea
and sat under a pine, watching the moon
so long his guest had to go and find him.
For Bashō, who first trudged
the road that led to the north,
who said his art was a furnace in summer
and a fan in winter, he was the poet,
the survivor of solitary winter
who carried kernels against the hope of spring,
and in him the hymn-singer seeking grace
humbly sings.

Rock

In Japan three hundred years ago
Bashō spoke of the diffident snow
over the hills of the far north,
where quail, I think, used to wander
and boys in groups went forth to track them.
His voice carries across the hills at night,
but there are no quail left there any more,
to track the snow, or call across the hills
to the boys in their camaraderie.
The snow itself melts into the streams in spring.
The rock, broken or dislodged, remains.
His voice, even at moments
when the brief spring touches it
with warmth, retains an echo
of men and nature locked
in love and struggle,
and therein its power,
and therefore, its grief.

<u>Stream</u>

When Bashō reached the Shirakawa gate,
opening to the northern regions,
the countryside was covered white
with thousands of flowers or early snow.
Neither priest nor man of the world
was he, but something in between,
doubtfully wavering the inland sea
between the bright and dark islands of night and day.
In a garden there, he heard
the mournful thock and plash
of a bamboo cistern in the stream,
filling up and spilling over, tipping
its water onto stone.
The stone became as ridged and smooth
as vulva and vagina.
In the midst of hauling hay
to the barn, aching with fatigue,
I sat down on a bale
and thought of it. That was years ago,
and in Vermont, where the short summer
peels away in fall.

Cloud

I watch you glaze a strawberry
with sugar, tilting your head over it
as we talk. It comes up in your hand
and disappears into your mouth.
The arc of the diver slipping into the sea
is no more beautiful to me.
The mountains tonight were veiled
in clouds, and became a presence,
like yours, in all my thoughts,
moving with me as I walked the field.
The dog ran and barked who now lies
asleep, murmuring dreams,
nose in the crook of her paws.

<u>Leaf</u>

On June 19, 1953
the Rosenbergs died, were murdered
by the State—a piece of ancient history,
and who remembers now, or cares to,
the cruelty of that date?
Like any of those days, perhaps,
in early summer, when leaves are still small and fresh
before their heaviness, and dappling sun
plays across the day, and school is finally
getting out, and music is released in streets.
They were victims, people say, of their time
and place, of McCarthy's ambition, Cold War
terror, and which of us can really say they were not guilty
of something? The Cold War's won,
and McCarthy is dead now, anyway.
But so are they.

<u>Moon</u>

I never shower alone in a house at night,
I don't know a woman who does.
Tonight is dark, without a moon, and rain
splatters against the screen.
This is the middle of the psychotic night
when every breath and heartbeat is magnified,
and I write. I wonder if any good
could come of it. But sometimes
when day has begun to break above the trees
and buildings lose their hoodedness,
I drive around and watch the people going to work.
There are so many of them, so many
who provide. Then the monster
will have to round again some other night,
heavily on exhausted feet.

<u>Beach</u>

The ancient Manyōshū poets
and those who sang in Provençal
bid you taste this morsel, fish,
lemon-scented, or that silken almond,
as you wish, and beckon you hear
the plucked music of koto and lute,
and gather together on some beach
where an ocean brushes the cool sand
in pale lights when the dawn rises.
We cannot think without language, and this too
is part of our world, the music which eases us
through night and cold, and through which
we express the pathos of lips on lips.
Come, Bashō. Eat. Sing.

You came to this peninsula and searched the cliffs
and every inlet in the bay. The sound, the one
you thought would save you, the one you are convinced
you traveled these miles for, waited with superhuman patience for,
really you'd been patient beyond belief, and then
at other times, frustrated in rage, were made to wait.
You knew it *would* save you, no doubt in your heart,
but you weren't sure what to listen for. You thought it was hiding,
it must be hiding, or hidden behind, the endless pillars of surf
endlessly crashing down, the seagulls' caws, the crash
of trees onto the forest floor, the gnashing of leaves
in storm. But perhaps it was not loud, it would come
on little feet, quietly, almost imperceptibly, when you had given up
listening and waiting and no longer expected it. It would come in
     peripheral vision,
in a sidelong way, smiling shyly as if to apologize. And you would
     recognize it at once.
It would come one way or the other, it had to but maybe you've missed
     it,
maybe it came and you were tired or not listening or asleep
and it came for only a second, less —how long is a sound?
It's too late and you're not saved you've missed your chance for sure
now you'll never be saved, but maybe not.

The field lies open, waiting.
Imprint your body upon it.
Be in its memory, sink. Let the weeds
overwhelm you, the long grass shade your face.
Let your legs lengthen into the afternoon.
The deer or rabbit may pay a visit, three pheasants come.
A green snake—harmless!—may sun on your belly.
Worms tunnel beneath you, roots plunge deeper.
Bees hum sweet music, honey music, bee music.
Look up, gaze into the other world.
Let space envelope you. You won't float in ether long,
gravity will keep you. We're all permanently tethered
to dirt. Let dirt clean you, birds pecking at seeds nick you.
Let summer lie on you as sun-shadow, cloud-shadow,
flight-shadow, green shadows lilt over you
and whisper behind your ear, "You've come." You've come this far.

Shenandoah, I love your daughter
and I know I'll never leave her.
She stands, straw hat in hand, laughing at me,
transparent skirts flowing around her,
sun on the back of her legs.
Lands of corn to the North,
to the South, delta
and her gesture, her joking voice
speak easily of exclusively feminine love.
Sapphic meters become her, the rhythms of water
surround her, I love her as water loves her as fluidity
soaks her as moisture fills me to the brim.
I would not dare to offend you, Mother,
who brings forth fruit of the plain, who brings her
into my sight. Her body dropping its veils
of water expresses my nakedness, my body illumines, and she
takes me in her mouth with the ease of a tigress
carries me, walking quietly through long grass. Surely I'm hers,
goodness and mercy follow me all the days of the earth
and she comforts me. Shenandoah, I love your daughter
and we lie down together. We love green sun,
ripe melons, singing, telling stories. Her hands
the color of chestnuts and mine the color of summer wheat
are suns thrilling skin, heat spreading
up through our thighs. My sight dims
in her blaze, her fingers score paths, copper, bronze, molten gold
on my skin. Each moment I grow wilder
as her eyes on me grow more and more calm.
In the stratosphere
the ancient cave-deer are leaping, in the hull of the earth
under great pressure
diamonds are forming from carbon.

She is open like a pool
but shy and I adore her.
Last night she almost leapt into my arms.
I was picking asters at the edge of the woods
in the last long hour of light, my kind of prayer
in the thick brush. No one could walk through it
without crashing. I heard her soft *click click*
and knew she was near and my ears went up.
As she entered the last leap into the open
she saw me. I caught a glimpse
of her tawny side, not three feet away, breast-high.
My arms went up and flew open wide.
Mid-air, she performed a perfect reverse jêté
and disappeared. I stared into the brush
a long time. It was as if
a perfect pool remained undisturbed,
as if nothing had happened, no blessing had passed
between us, no blue flowers were spread on the ground.

SUNDAY MORNING

They all think I'm a man, and take a long second look,
or listen closely to my voice, before they apologize.
In the East, that mistake would make them sullen
or mean, with no apology offered.
I can't decide what does it—my haircut, pants, walk,
my sports car—I don't know why this should be my problem
and not their own, but it nags.

                        An outsider passing through, in a café
somewhere in South Dakota. No one
actually says hello, but they note my appearance
with care. The look that takes in my car
with plates from far out of state, my gentle
indoor dog, my city clothes.
Then the brief nod of acknowledgment.

I listen to their conversation, more from boredom
than real interest, and they know I listen.
Every few minutes I catch an eye
which quickly slides away. Hardworking,
hardscrabble people, for the most part, poor.
Some of the men are uncommonly handsome—
in fact, Yves Montand smokes in the next booth—
but the women! The beautiful ones
must have used their beauty like currency
in order to get out. The others
had little to spend, but they could work.
It's their work that makes them valuable
and traps them here.

                        I am most polite to the waitress,
thanking the coffee, the eggs and toast,
thanking profusely the newspaper, and tip too well,
thinking I don't want to be shot on the way out of town.
I feel I know them but they don't know me,
and the plains are theirs. Last night
I stood alone somewhere out on those plains,
the rush of winds gathered from miles away in my ears,

the crickets going mad lickety-split. Two days here
and already I feel myself freezing back and down
to that ice age which glacially carved this land.
If only I were a believer, this place
would make my faith fail.

                          In Idaho
they sell silver at every stop, in Montana
it's copper, here in Dakota, rocks.
Pushing ninety, I begin to pass a car
but the woman in it captures my eye.
She crouches in the driver's seat but faces the rear.
Her eyes fall hard on mine, brittle
with contempt, but her mouth
is on the driver's, whose face is blocked.
I recognize, without being able to see,
exactly how her hands move on him
below the window. I can see from her face
I am meant to be shocked by this dexterous
high-speed display, but instead I only want
to get by in the moment before he comes.
I grip the wheel and floor it.

V.
Catastrophe Theory

CATASTROPHE THEORY
For Barbara Herrnstein Smith

This morning, frost clung to everything:
wrinkled apples
still hanging on a bare-branched tree,
field, broken with stalks,
blades of grass, silver
where sunlight glints off them.
Smeared white mountains in the distance,
women's shapes, lying in soft light.

Yet it is warm. A woman walks the field
with her dog, wondering at the earth,
its slow curving fall from morning to night,
its birth and death, invisible, indivisible
from life, from its own recent summer and its fruit,
from her changing body and her scarf.

Last summer, she sat with a friend
by a Southern stream, mourning, talking of children,
forests, the polar ice caps, warming,
fires, birds and fish giving warning.
Catastrophe theory—the idea that accidents can occur in such a way
they create new means and forms, something like pearls—
may regain life for the earth, another billion years
of insects and fish, small species, trees.

She walks the field, head down, as if searching.
The dog thrusts its nose into frost-white leaves.

Late autumn rains
have given the garden a terrible hangover. Chrysanthemums
stand withered near the door, in the beds
the vegetables are reduced to stalks.
I watch the bay. When Liu Yung
suffered, she came here to watch the water
and wander the back roads which all stop at the cliffs.
She stayed in this empty house
until the cold winds came, fogs over the waters,
crickets chattering back and forth,
enough to drive anyone mad.

Change comes glacially. The night
brings the Milky Way and the moon, transparent
as the memory of silk on her breasts. Thought follows thought,
night after night, the years wound me.
I squandered years hanging around the city.
Oh, the city was fine! Eating all night, drinking all day,
young women kissing and toasting each other,
lingering near the music until late, then pairing off.
Those days! Since then, time's clacked by
like a shuttle. Hidden here in the mists,
I'll go on.

                       She's an awkward draftswoman,
and this makes her horses peculiar. She'll draw the body
oddly elongated, a too-small head. Inevitably, weak lines for the
   haunches,
in the zone where hips slope down sharply, squeeze in to upper legs.
But then she'll make a marker, the marker for *horse*,
in the chest, the powerful shoulders, or the hooves, planted exactly.
Still, they're strange horses. They look recently unearthed,
from the past, the mire of time. They evoke their own lineage, far back
to the Rowiche horse, which galloped through grasslands at the head of
   the Mekong.
The source of the Mekong was found, only last year, in Mongolia.
The Rowiche horse had not been known to exist. It's small but sturdy.
So came Mongolian warriors, speed-riding expertly without saddles,
cave-dwelling artists in southern France and northern Spain,
and pictograph-makers living in cliffs in the American Southwest.
Possibly they—the horses, I mean, though I could as easily speak
of the riders and artists—they're buried far back in consciousness,
or in dream. Possibly —they could be—about human memory and
   longing,
since we don't know about horse memory and longing.

                    However, in Rothenberg
there is never a rider. And there's little color, the palette being stringent,
though red's in it. Black and white, the less ethereal, more steely blues.
A strong band or X is often superimposed, as if barring or crossing
the horse's path. In which case the horse is about to crash into it.
But as often the horse stands perfectly still, either facing or in profile.
And everything is scumbled, line, shape, color—just like life!
As if a memory were emerging slowly, the elements not yet
fully intact. Or a photograph swimming in the unearthly light
of the darkroom. The lack of particular background, except
as a zone of scumbled color, makes the horses appear to float.
Especially when the background is white, with numerous depths
layers and scorings, a color that can only be called *whitish*.
A vapor, a fog, thick gaseous air. Like astronauts floating in space,
linked with the universe, then abandoned in it.

Now, Amelia, when moonlight blanches the leaves
in their sonorous thousands, you might be
the subject of someone's art.
Hopper's woman, dressed in distinctive white,
caught on a headland above the ocean, turning—
toward what? Or whom?
At the center of Turner's vortex, in a swirl of flame.
In Munch's painting, a woman standing
at the rail of a boat, hands risen to face, her scream,
its mad, resounding "O"
pressed murderously on a nerve.
No, this: Hopper's etching:
the sleeper awakened, nude,
who bends before a window
where curtains catch the breeze
on passionate, abandoned sheets.

The moon, like us, is beautifully deceptive in her tricks.
She whispers and rustles the leaves, making you think, or feel,
that someone walks there. Surely a man.
Approaching your window. But you are no man's art.
And I have shared those sheets.
If you sit in bed in the afternoon, writing letters, or paint
where bark came off the cherry in your garden,
or enter a seminar to speak of Pemberly and Howards End,
is this failure? Is it failure when men follow you with their eyes
but never approach? Is it failure, to love your students?
Are you a failure, loving my breasts, my mouth,
my labia opening to your lips?

You would pursue the argument bleakly through
to its end in some dogged, daylit room.
I've made my commitment, to one kind of love
and to you. You worry and waver and beg to disagree,
while leaves continue to whisper, harsh, brutally cruel,
failure failure failure failure. Miserable failure.
Your judgments haunt you at morning, even as,
at night, your whole body trembling, you plead
and I enter and you cry out. Night after night after night.

"On the first flight, two women,
twenty and twenty-two;
on the second, this sixty-five-year-old woman
and the sixteen-year-old boy.
Unconscious, drugged, but still alive."
I am reading a poem, called "Spring Drawing."
"I threw them out the open door."
It has lilacs in it, lilacs against white houses.
I am in a white house, coped with black shutters, and lilacs
taller than a man stand in the yard.
"We were far out over the ocean.
"Once, I fell and almost slipped out myself."
Handfuls of crocus have opened
by the stone wall. The lilacs will flower
in June. Here, they are still only stick figures.
"Afterward, I slept until five the next
afternoon." The poet lives in California,
where spring draws out blooms in February
and March. I live far to the east and north. A painting
by Pierre Bonnard lavishes the cover of his book.
"Then I drank two whiskeys,
sought out the chaplain
who said I had not done wrong."
The painting shows an open window, green
panes against red interior walls. *"It was not a sin,*
he told me, they had had a Christian death."
The open window frames the view:
masses of leaves, partial sky a cloudless blue,
bamboo shade, thin, like a peignoir
that encourages one's gaze on breasts.
"It was a war, the dirty war.
"They were subversives, the chaplain said."
He is the poet of childhood, of recollected
grace, the gorgeous taste of blackberries.
"Lilacs against white houses,
two sparrows, one streaked—"
A minute ago came a finch,
dull yellow feathers, still bundled in winter clothes.
I put down the book and walk across the room.

I stand in a beautiful house,
with clean symmetrical windows flooding light.
"That is how they were disappeared.
"I disappeared them.
"I have permanent punishment now."

The House

Weak afternoon light leans on the house
opposite, shutters change from black to green.
It's not a change of season, but the season
deepens and becomes more itself. January.
I know this house as a person,
it too has received letters, been loved
and then unloved. The frames of the windows,
gray as the winter Atlantic, have been telling me
they know something about emptiness.

When I entered my steps rang in the rooms
with a sharp report.
On the floor were scattered: a ball of string,
cans of paint, plumb-line chalk, milky blue.
I felt like plunging my whole hand in paint
and pressing my palm high on the wall, fingers spread,
to mark my presence as they once did in the ancient caves,
one handprint red, one in black. A few charging horses.
After I leave, the rooms murmur again.
The lilacs by the walk stand watch
near the entrance after light fades from the porch.

LINEAR

After a poem by Mary Leader

I came out of solitude, driving from desert
and plains to this valley, so unlike the one
recently left, and these low mountains, whose line at night
is like the silhouette of a woman. A woman no longer young,
heavy in the hips and with pendulous breasts;
or like an old statue, fallen on its side, lying in weeds.
To this river in which leaves raft, barely moving,
gold, red, gold, in the midst, the mist of mornings.
But I didn't, couldn't expect—

how, after pain, plenitude comes. At night, here,
have you noticed the colors slip-shifting among ranges of grays?
How the cloud of the Pleiades fogs sight and breath?
How, in the line of the woods, the trees and shrubs
stand still, like granite shapes? Like a deer
slip-stepping at night from woods
into field, you appeared. Your face, alert,
subtly changing as if you are thinking, hard.

I'm reminded of Bashō, who went to fetch water for tea
and sat under a pine, watching the moon so long
his guest had to go and find him. I am that guest,
and this is your place, you've made it yours
through brutal nights of weaving and weeping.
You stand in the garden and the brittle crusts
of leaves stop crumbling.
A frost of leaves veils the grass;
moonlight falls, a cloak on your shoulders.
I note the shapes of the shrubs and trees, the way they're spaced
behind you. You appear to be listening.
Nostrils shift, sensing, searching. For dangers?
Is it dangerous for you, if I'm here?
We are quiet, as distinct
and separate from each other as trees.
I'm not ready, wasn't prepared, not for your presence,
not for desire I thought extinguished, I wasn't prepared
to feel again, every part of me united by one idea.

96

I must find the structure for this situation.
Find the right relation of body to mind, of my body
to yours, the right alignment of trees like dolmen stones
facing the universe, the right relation of stone to desire.
Step toward you. A remark is needed; I make it.
"This moonlight reminds me of Bashō." You glance at me,
appraising. Clouds wash the lunar surface, drenched
in otherworldly light. I am breathing hard, but barely.
To calm you. I have to work and this is hard labor, work
without letting you know I am working.

                                  I point, casually,
taking a neat half-step toward you as if in order to direct
your eye. "The Pleiades. There." You seem to relax.
We don't know each other, nothing here is of consequence,
we might have moved away from a party or some reception
briefly and for no other reason than to inhale the air.
Happened to meet, out in the garden. The white
and gray shapes, dove, mauve and charcoal shading to black,
the shadows of trees and shrubs sluice the moonlight.
Only night is between us. So I could tell myself if I chose.

I swallow, my mouth has gone dry. I must keep you here
if only briefly—so briefly and noncommitally it will not register
and you will not think of it afterwards, alone or with someone in your
    room.
I must be here I think I will die without it, but not *here with you.*
I'm transgressing, not only against the rule of touch,
                                    entirely untested,
I'm under a more formidable ban. The thought of a kiss
can't become a kiss. The words *I want you* must not be uttered.

For if, for even one second,
I lift my lips, tip towards you, even one inch, that inch
could collapse the meter between us, the thin span
—so slight we can't even see it—between us, tear.
High on the balls of my feet I'd reach for—nothing.
I'd spook you back into woods. Your face would slip,
yanked away,
it would disappear.

                                        I don't want
to stand separate for one more minute. I can't bring myself
toward you, not a quarter-inch more than I have,
don't dare, I can't close the final distance between us.
You are speaking, a husky voice, unaware of its
beautiful modulations, and the structure of a sentence
as it unfolds from your mouth, hesitates, continues,
thrills me. I focus on your mouth, my whole body
tenses, leans forward, centered on your lips.
You look at me full-faced and smile.

I'm flooded. I smile back, tilt as if dazed,
fainting, I can barely stand, tip toward you,
think I am going to fall, if we come together and meet
it will be because I have fallen into you as you stand.
You are looking at me, a little bewildered.
A space opens while I try to find equilibrium.

"Well. I'm pretty tired. I've got to go."
A decision you won't remember.
You speak politely, a slight tilt of the head.
Sideways, not in my direction. I notice the gold earring
half-hidden in your hair. "Sure. Of course."
I knew you would leave. You are going.
"Good night."
"Yes. *Good night.*"

This is how I can prevent your going, prevent
calling your name. Memorize:
the fingers as you gestured, palms down,
the smile as you spoke, memorize your legs,
your gait, the way you hold your head and shoulders as you move,
now memorize the moonlight, shining on leaves,
how you move like a deer
across and through long shadows.
                        Note
the line of the woods, the shrubs, granite shapes
in the shades of darkness, darkness merging with darkness.
Vertical pines, horizontal shadows, charcoal stripes across ground.
Memorize sky, the fog of stars, how they join.
I know you will not remember this less-than-half-an-hour
by the time you undress, alone or with someone
in your room. I shut my eyes.

VI.
Hyakutake

In memory of my mother, Roma P. Basile, 1915–1992

My Winter Vacation

I flew out of the mountains
at racing speed from Montana into Idaho,
hands on the wheel at ten and two o'clock,
straightening the curves for greater speed,
nothing for miles but noise and wind, me in my car
and the herds of mule deer descending the mountainsides
under a placid azure sky. All change and time
had stopped for you, while I rocketed through
making a beeline for my place in Seattle.

I had no love, only the need that turned my heart
at midnight into a hollow pumpkin, and
while I sadly envisioned the one woman—the only one—
saxophones behind a white man's wailing voice,
she was elsewhere. I made sure
I was elsewhere when you were dying,
sick as I was of the slow round robin
from nursing home to hospital crisis and back,
the universal hell for chronic cases, those
for whom no hope can possibly linger in those smells,
the daily drone punctuated by moans and curses—I was
fleeing in desperation for quiet and a breath of air.
I used to feel a deepening hole deepen again
whenever you had another seizure or infection,
because it meant you might finally die.

Even the constant rain became a relief, soft
as a pillow and as sweet. The bamboo
in the Japanese garden on Madison
mooed softly in the winter green, all spinach
and white light and wetness in the early descending dark.
I sat alone and sipped yet another cappuccino
down East Denny hill at the buzzing B&O.
I was always alone in Seattle, it was my place
to be alone, and apart from my rounds
to Red & Black and Elliott Bay and Bailey/Coy,
and daily hits at Bulldog News and Starbuck's counter
looking out at Broadway, it wasn't much.

A quiet place, nothing happens there, which is what
I wanted, for nothing to happen forever.
You could vegetate and be babied till the end of time,
while the Space Needle winked back in my kitchen at night,
monotonous as your machines, one blink red, one blink green.
One blink red—

                                        No, that wasn't true.
I wanted you to die, but you wouldn't. You held on and on
until I began to plot your death, the tubes ripped out
some night, late, the possibilities of a large pillow.
I stole my father's twenty-two—by then I couldn't have said
whether I would use it on myself, or you.
Finally, one gray cotton-wool day
he called and said you had an infection.
Would I come back? I didn't need to pack.
I got on a plane and spoke to no one,
consuming those little bottles of Scotch
as I watched schools of clouds below us
flash-fire into the orange globe of the sun,
the western half of the heavens a charging pulse of light,
the other half, the one I was flying to at jet-speed in the dark.

THE GARDEN

For my part
we are as we were
across the table that afternoon:
your pleasure in opening a gift. . . .
It was May, toward the end.
You, at seventy, like a pond where trees lay down their long bodies
after travail, in shadows.

For years I tried to find the plates
with lemon yellow borders
like Monet's
to give to you.

A simple lunch: a pear, some cheese,
strawberries, then back to work
in your blue worker's coat, gloves, old shoes.
In summer you would forget to come in for dinner.
Your work, your garden, expanding
and continually replanted with banks
of this or that, a little something-or-other
in its special spot. You so loved sunny corners;
planned a silver garden within the garden,
a cutting garden, herbs, the placement of a rock,
a path. Always changing, adding,
a Japanese lamp, a bamboo pipe of water
falling into a stone basin, something for the new season
as the old season turned, a celebration
or surprise. Tearing up whole beds and starting again.

I learned this work from you,
shaping, revising, the art of juxtaposition;
the weather and the season
continuously changing,
full of death and sorrow. Then mysteriously renewed.

A jagged country of bays and inlets, rock-jetties, cliffs,
a smuggler's coast. The wide-bodied pine, the madrona
which never sheds its leaves, the Douglas fir have all been scorched
by fires. The first fires were made by Indians on the beach,
to hollow logs for canoes, to smoke their great catches
of salmon and crab. Beach-rubble is strewn everywhere—
trees crashed down the cliffs in storms, logs
washed up, rags of kelp and seaweed,
beds of shattered shells and sea-borne stones,
driftwood, riprap, junk. Nothing is whole,
everything's partial or simply, waste.
It's a country of waste. Clear-cutting has shaved
whole sides of mountains, and you can't go half an hour
on land in any direction without passing fields of stumps.

The same waste on the prairies: burn-marks, scars from machines,
rusted wire, fence-posts attached to air, houses with sky where roof
    should be.
Every so often—frequently, in fact—death at the side of the road:
a white cross, two, a cluster, with plastic bouquets.

The waste is chilling, and it rains dark here,
dark as the mornings are white with fog. The days seep open,
everything I own is infected with damp. I feel hung up, wrung out,
broken out here on the edge of the Western world.
Dusks, I've taken to standing on a promontory, facing Japan,
looking out to where ocean and sky become seamless.

My mother's grave is this ocean.
I didn't think of her when I came to this coast.
I only walked and studied the surf.
But now I've remembered something—a bit funny, odd,
uncomfortable-funny. After the stroke, when I knew
she was dying, I went out of my way to find her birthplace.
A tiny town, two thousand miles inland.

The star returns and pierces once, here,
at the tail-end of winter, at the anniversary
of my mother's death. It would seem that God,
sitting in Her blackened sky, surrounded
by the seraphim stars, acknowledges this
by sending the messenger Comet Hyakutake.
But no. God died, circa 1962;
or has turned away, indifferent
to my little grief; or can't hear as well
as She once did. So this shadowy smudge
of ice, gas and dust, returning as it does
once in 10,000 years, is only another
phenomenon, like Elvis's claimed return
or the discovery of Hitler, alive
and living with Eva Braun in Argentina.
In the cold the branches snap
and crackle, and snowfields give off
an unearthly glow all the way from Virgo
to Perseus. The star-snow
of space, as I stand in the field looking up,
is like facing eternity alone. Alone
and speechless, as my mother was
when death carried her, high up
and away from us in a shrouded sky,
but refused either to claim her or set her down.
She died in the dreadful season
before Easter, and when Easter came,
there was no one. Hosannas went up,
celebrations took place, prayers were answered
elsewhere, God's breath warmed some other
earth than this, another galaxy burst open,
and the seraphim stars whose light cut clear through here
into the frozen earth, saw my little stick figure
standing in a snowfield, and the billions of other
stick figures, winked at each other
knowingly, and continued to look on.

Adrian Oktenberg is the author of *The Bosnia Elegies* (1997) and a chapbook, *Drawing in the Dirt*. She has won the Astraea Lesbian Writer's Award, the *Americas Review* poetry prize, grants from the Barbara Deming Fund and the Massachusetts Cultural Council, and The Philip Roth Residency at Bucknell University. Her work has appeared in many journals including *Prairie Schooner*, *New Letters*, *Ploughshares*, *The Kenyon Review*, *Luna* and *The American Voice*. She has been a regular contributor to *The Women's Review of Books* since 1983.